THE BROWN FIXER
MONEY MANAGER

T.R.A.C Publishing
P.O Box 1243
Austell, GA 30168

Copyright © 2016 Shakisha Edness
No part of this book can be reproduced without written permission from the author.

ISBN – 13: 9781536958003
ISBN – 10: 153695800X

For Inquiries Contact Shakisha Edness
507 - 405 - 4742

INTRODUCTION

This is designed to help those who need help with managing their finances. You may be working with a little or a lot; but you are tired of living from paycheck to paycheck.

Whatever you let get out of order, will soon be out of your control.

Get total control of your finances by telling it where to go and what to do! Get control NOW!

THE BROWN FIXER MONEY MANAGER

YOU NEED THE FOLLOWING:

- Calculator.
- Calendar (Included).
- Two different color highlighters.
- ALL of your bills (Financial responsibilities).
- A month's worth of paystubs (Four paystubs/weekly or two paystubs/biweekly).
- If it's an income that comes in on an ongoing basis, it can be counted (Child-support, retirement, disability check etc.).
- Checking and savings account statements (only the month prior to you starting The Brown Fixer).

YOU WILL NEED TO DO THE FOLLOWING:

1. Write down EVERYTHING you pay during the month (Ex: Rent, Phone, Light, Water, Gas, Life/Car Ins., Credit cards, Cellular phone, Gas (in the car), Lawn care, Household supplies, Personal hygiene supplies, Haircuts, Manicure & Pedicure). EVERYTHING!

LIST BILLS	DUE DATE	AMOUNT
RENT/MORTGAGE		
PHONE		
LIGHT		
WATER		
GAS		
LIFE/CAR INS		
FIRE/THEFT		
CABLE		
TRASH		
LAWN CARE		
PET CARE		
MANICURE/PEDICURE		
HAIRCUT/HAIR		
FOOD		
CREDIT CARD		
LOAN		
CAR NOTE		
COPAYS		
HEALTH INS		
CHILD CARE		
AFTER SCHOOL CARE		
		TOTAL

LIST BILLS	DUE DATE	AMOUNT

Extra Columns for Extra Bills

2. Then, add the sum of all your bills.
3. After adding up all of your bills, add up your INCOME for the month. INCOME means EVERYTHING that's COMING IN!

INCOMING INCOME	DATE RECEIVE	AMOUNT

Now you are aware of what's coming in and what's going out, and what you have LEFT!

4. Separate the bills by categorizing them by their dates. Ex: 1, 5, & 9 and 13, 18, & 20. The purpose is to place the bills that are close in numbers together, so you can KNOW what paycheck is designated to pay those bills.

LIST BILLS	DUE DATE

5. Now take the calendar and write PAY DAY for each time you get paid and/or receive any other INCOME COMING IN on an ONGOING BASIS. You can write that on the calendar referencing the day you expect to receive it.

6. Write the bills on the calendar as well. Now this makes it easier for you to decide which check will pay which bill, ON TIME or BEFORE TIME! Remember we do NOT pay late!

MONTH YEAR

MONDAY	TUESDAY	WEDNESDAY	THURSDAY	FRIDAY	SATURDAY	SUNDAY
☐	☐	☐	☐	☐	☐	☐
☐	☐	☐	☐	☐	☐	☐
☐	☐	☐	☐	☐	☐	☐
☐	☐	☐	☐	☐	☐	☐
☐	☐	☐	☐	☐	☐	☐
☐	☐	☐	☐	☐	☐	☐

Manually write the information on the calendar depending on when you start.

7. Now that you have a system in place of ADDING UP what COMES IN and SUBTRACTING what GOES OUT; now you can decide what amount you would like to save. Then DECIDE the DATE that you want to ACCOMPLISH your GOAL.

8. DETERMINE the amount you will SAVE on a weekly or biweekly basis. This should come DIRECTLY from your check INTO your SAVINGS ACCOUNT.

9. After you DECIDE the amount that you are DETERMINED to SAVE, you must DECIDE on the amount to be withdrawn from both checks. This is setting a plan up to WIN not fail!

10. Go to HR and request a direct deposit form and fill it out. This is how you SCHEDULE IT!

GOAL AMOUNT TO SAVE	GOAL ACCOMPLISH DATE
SCHEDULED DATES	**SCHEDULED AMOUNTS**

In your own words write why you want to save the above amount. You must know the "reason why" in order to stay the course. This serves as a reminder to you in case you get off of track.

_____
_____
_____
_____
_____
_____
_____
_____

Finalized Plan

INCOMING	OUTGOING	LEFT	SAVINGS	MISC.

Below is a monthly spending plan chart. It will help keep track of all of your monthly purchases.

PURCHASE	DATE OF PURCHASE	AMOUNT OF PURCHASE

Helpful Tips:

- Flat Rate Billing – Budget systems with your utility bills.
- Checking and Savings Accounts NOT combined.
- No Debit Card for your Savings Account.
- Preferably*Savings account with Credit Union.
- Child support in an entire different account.

1 Thessalonians 5:18 In everything give thanks: for this is the Will of God in Christ Jesus concerning you.

In some cases, we can't give thanks for everything. Maybe because everything is not good; but even in the bad GIVE THANKS! God says, the Good and the Bad will work out for your Good.

Matthew 25:21 The Master said, "Well done my Good & Faithful Servant. You have been FAITHFUL in HANDLING this SMALL amount, so NOW I will GIVE you MANY MORE RESPONSIBILITIES. Let's CELEBRATE Together!

We must also learn how to be FAITHFUL for the small things, because if not we cannot be trusted with more. God wants to see how FAITHFUL we are with MANAGING the little, so He can TRUST us with MORE Responsibilities.

- Manage = Direct Control (To be in charge of).
- Optimize = Make the BEST use of. (Most effective of).
- Navigate = Plan & Direct the route. (Create a Financial Route Plan) A way to get from one place to another.
- Examine & Execute = Test the knowledge /Carry out & put into effect. (The Plan).
- Yield = Produce & Provide. The income returns on the investment cost.

- You must be in charge over your finances and have direct control over it! Do NOT let anyone else control your finances unless it's someone that has your best interest.
- Learn how to put your money to its best use, refrain from spending it foolishly!
- You must have a Financial Route Plan telling it where to go and what to do. The plan is to help you get from where you are to where you are going.
- Just as you have to go get an examination once a year, I advise you to Examine your finances as well. Make sure the plan you set in place is working for you. If it is not, make some adjustments.
- "Produce and provide" simply explains that every investment should schedule a return.

YOU WILL NEED TO DO THE FOLLOWING:

1. Write down EVERYTHING you pay during the month (Ex: Rent, Phone, Light, Water, Gas, Life/Car Ins., Credit cards, Cellular phone, Gas (in the car), Lawn care, Household supplies, Personal hygiene supplies, Haircuts, Manicure & Pedicure). EVERYTHING!

LIST BILLS	DUE DATE	AMOUNT
RENT/MORTGAGE		
PHONE		
LIGHT		
WATER		
GAS		
LIFE/CAR INS		
FIRE/THEFT		
CABLE		
TRASH		
LAWN CARE		
PET CARE		
MANICURE/PEDICURE		
HAIRCUT/HAIR		
FOOD		
CREDIT CARD		
LOAN		
CAR NOTE		
COPAYS		
HEALTH INS		
CHILD CARE		
AFTER SCHOOL CARE		
		TOTAL

LIST BILLS	DUE DATE	AMOUNT

Extra Columns for Extra Bills

2. Then, add the sum of all your bills.
3. After adding up all of your bills, add up your INCOME for the month. INCOME means EVERYTHING that's COMING IN!

INCOMING INCOME	DATE RECEIVE	AMOUNT

Now you are aware of what's coming in and what's going out, and what you have LEFT!

4. Separate the bills by categorizing them by their dates. Ex: 1, 5, & 9 and 13, 18, & 20. The purpose is to place the bills that are close in numbers together, so you can KNOW what paycheck is designated to pay those bills.

LIST BILLS	DUE DATE

5. Now take the calendar and write PAY DAY for each time you get paid and/or receive any other INCOME COMING IN on an ONGOING BASIS. You can write that on the calendar referencing the day you expect to receive it.

6. Write the bills on the calendar as well. Now this makes it easier for you to decide which check will pay which bill, ON TIME or BEFORE TIME! Remember we do NOT pay late!

MONTH YEAR

MONDAY	TUESDAY	WEDNESDAY	THURSDAY	FRIDAY	SATURDAY	SUNDAY
☐	☐	☐	☐	☐	☐	☐
☐	☐	☐	☐	☐	☐	☐
☐	☐	☐	☐	☐	☐	☐
☐	☐	☐	☐	☐	☐	☐
☐	☐	☐	☐	☐	☐	☐
☐	☐	☐	☐	☐	☐	☐

Manually write the information on the calendar depending on when you start.

7. Now that you have a system in place of ADDING UP what COMES IN and SUBTRACTING what GOES OUT; Now you can decide what amount you would like to save. Then DECIDE the DATE that you want to ACCOMPLISH your GOAL.

8. DETERMINE the amount you will SAVE on a weekly or biweekly basis. This should come DIRECTLY from your check INTO your SAVINGS ACCOUNT.

9. After you DECIDE the amount that you are DETERMINED to SAVE, you must DECIDE on the amount to be withdrawn from both checks. This is setting a plan up to WIN not fail!

10. Go to HR and request a direct deposit form and fill it out. This is how you SCHEDULE IT!

GOAL AMOUNT TO SAVE	GOAL ACCOMPLISH DATE
SCHEDULED DATES	**SCHEDULED AMOUNTS**

In your own words write why you want to save the above amount. You must know the "reason why" in order to stay the course. This serves as a reminder to you in case you get off of track.

_____
_____
_____
_____
_____
_____
_____
_____

Finalized Plan

INCOMING	OUTGOING	LEFT	SAVINGS	MISC.

Below is a monthly spending plan chart. It will help keep track of all of your monthly purchases.

PURCHASE	DATE OF PURCHASE	AMOUNT OF PURCHASE

Helpful Tips:

- Flat Rate Billing – Budget systems with your utility bills.
- Checking and Savings Accounts NOT combined.
- No Debit Card for your Savings Account.
- Preferably*Savings account with Credit Union.
- Child support in an entire different account.

1 Thessalonians 5:18 In everything give thanks: for this is the Will of God in Christ Jesus concerning you.

In some cases, we can't give thanks for everything. Maybe because everything is not good; but even in the bad GIVE THANKS! God says, the Good and the Bad will work out for your Good.

Matthew 25:21 The Master said, "Well done my Good & Faithful Servant. You have been FAITHFUL in HANDLING this SMALL amount, so NOW I will GIVE you MANY MORE RESPONSIBILITIES. Let's CELEBRATE Together!

We must also learn how to be FAITHFUL for the small things, because if not we cannot be trusted with more. God wants to see how FAITHFUL we are with MANAGING the little, so He can TRUST us with MORE Responsibilities.

- Manage = Direct Control (To be in charge of).
- Optimize = Make the BEST use of. (Most effective of).
- Navigate = Plan & Direct the route. (Create a Financial Route Plan) A way to get from one place to another.
- Examine & Execute = Test the knowledge /Carry out & put into effect. (The Plan).
- Yield = Produce & Provide. The income returns on the investment cost.

- You must be in charge over your finances and have direct control over it! Do NOT let anyone else control your finances unless it's someone that has your best interest.
- Learn how to put your money to its best use, refrain from spending it foolishly!
- You must have a Financial Route Plan telling it where to go and what to do. The plan is to help you get from where you are to where you are going.
- Just as you have to go get an examination once a year, I advise you to Examine your finances as well. Make sure the plan you set in place is working for you. If it is not, make some adjustments.
- "Produce and provide" simply explains that every investment should schedule a return.

YOU WILL NEED TO DO THE FOLLOWING:

1. Write down EVERYTHING you pay during the month Ex: Rent, Phone, Light, Water, Gas, Life/Car Ins., Credit cards, Cellular phone, Gas (in the car), Lawn care, Household supplies, Personal hygiene supplies, Haircuts, Manicure & Pedicure). EVERYTHING!

LIST BILLS	DUE DATE	AMOUNT
RENT/MORTGAGE		
PHONE		
LIGHT		
WATER		
GAS		
LIFE/CAR INS		
FIRE/THEFT		
CABLE		
TRASH		
LAWN CARE		
PET CARE		
MANICURE/PEDICURE		
HAIRCUT/HAIR		
FOOD		
CREDIT CARD		
LOAN		
CAR NOTE		
COPAYS		
HEALTH INS		
CHILD CARE		
AFTER SCHOOL CARE		
		TOTAL

LIST BILLS	DUE DATE	AMOUNT

Extra Columns for Extra Bills

2. Then, add the sum of all your bills.
3. After adding up all of your bills, add up your INCOME for the month. INCOME means EVERYTHING that's COMING IN!

INCOMING INCOME	DATE RECEIVE	AMOUNT

Now you are aware of what's coming in and what's going out, and what you have LEFT!

4. Separate the bills by categorizing them by their dates. Ex: 1, 5, & 9 and 13, 18, & 20. The purpose is to place the bills that are close in numbers together, so you can KNOW what paycheck is designated to pay those bills.

LIST BILLS	DUE DATE

5. Now take the calendar and write PAY DAY for each time you get paid and/or receive any other INCOME COMING IN on an ONGOING BASIS. You can write that on the calendar referencing the day you expect to receive it.

6. Write the bills on the calendar as well. Now this makes it easier for you to decide which check will pay which bill, ON TIME or BEFORE TIME! Remember we do NOT pay late!

MONTH YEAR

MONDAY	TUESDAY	WEDNESDAY	THURSDAY	FRIDAY	SATURDAY	SUNDAY
☐	☐	☐	☐	☐	☐	☐
☐	☐	☐	☐	☐	☐	☐
☐	☐	☐	☐	☐	☐	☐
☐	☐	☐	☐	☐	☐	☐
☐	☐	☐	☐	☐	☐	☐
☐	☐	☐	☐	☐	☐	☐

Manually write the information on the calendar depending on when you start.

7. Now that you have a system in place of ADDING UP what COMES IN and SUBTRACTING what GOES OUT; Now you can decide what amount you would like to save. Then DECIDE the DATE that you want to ACCOMPLISH your GOAL.

8. DETERMINE the amount you will SAVE on a weekly or biweekly basis. This should come DIRECTLY from your check INTO your SAVINGS ACCOUNT.

9. After you DECIDE the amount that you are DETERMINED to SAVE, you must DECIDE on the amount to be withdrawn from both checks. This is setting a plan up to WIN not fail!

10. Go to HR and request a direct deposit form and fill it out. This is how you SCHEDULE IT!

GOAL AMOUNT TO SAVE	GOAL ACCOMPLISH DATE
SCHEDULED DATES	**SCHEDULED AMOUNTS**

In your own words write why you want to save the above amount. You must know the "reason why" in order to stay the course. This serves as a reminder to you in case you get off of track.

_____
_____
_____
_____
_____
_____
_____
_____

Finalized Plan

INCOMING	OUTGOING	LEFT	SAVINGS	MISC.

Below is a monthly spending plan chart. It will help keep track of all of your monthly purchases.

PURCHASE	DATE OF PURCHASE	AMOUNT OF PURCHASE

Helpful Tips:

- Flat Rate Billing – Budget systems with your utility bills.
- Checking and Savings Accounts NOT combined.
- No Debit Card for your Savings Account.
- Preferably*Savings account with Credit Union.
- Child support in an entire different account.

1 Thessalonians 5:18 In everything give thanks: for this is the Will of God in Christ Jesus concerning you.

In some cases, we can't give thanks for everything. Maybe because everything is not good; but even in the bad GIVE THANKS! God says, the Good and the Bad will work out for your Good.

Matthew 25:21 The Master said, "Well done my Good & Faithful Servant. You have been FAITHFUL in HANDLING this SMALL amount, so NOW I will GIVE you MANY MORE RESPONSIBILITIES. Let's CELEBRATE Together!

We must also learn how to be FAITHFUL for the small things, because if not we cannot be trusted with more. God wants to see how FAITHFUL we are with MANAGING the little, so He can TRUST us with MORE Responsibilities.

- Manage = Direct Control (To be in charge of).
- Optimize = Make the BEST use of. (Most effective of).
- Navigate = Plan & Direct the route. (Create a Financial Route Plan) A way to get from one place to another.
- Examine & Execute = Test the knowledge /Carry out & put into effect. (The Plan).
- Yield = Produce & Provide. The income returns on the investment cost.

- You must be in charge over your finances and have direct control over it! Do NOT let anyone else control your finances unless it's someone that has your best interest.
- Learn how to put your money to its best use, refrain from spending it foolishly!
- You must have a Financial Route Plan telling it where to go and what to do. The plan is to help you get from where you are to where you are going.
- Just as you have to go get an examination once a year, I advise you to Examine your finances as well. Make sure the plan you set in place is working for you. If it is not, make some adjustments.
- "Produce and provide" simply explains that every investment should schedule a return.

YOU WILL NEED TO DO THE FOLLOWING:

1. Write down EVERYTHING you pay during the month (Ex: Rent, Phone, Light, Water, Gas, Life/Car Ins., Credit cards, Cellular phone, Gas (in the car), Lawn care, Household supplies, Personal hygiene supplies, Haircuts, Manicure & Pedicure). EVERYTHING!

LIST BILLS	DUE DATE	AMOUNT
RENT/MORTGAGE		
PHONE		
LIGHT		
WATER		
GAS		
LIFE/CAR INS		
FIRE/THEFT		
CABLE		
TRASH		
LAWN CARE		
PET CARE		
MANICURE/PEDICURE		
HAIRCUT/HAIR		
FOOD		
CREDIT CARD		
LOAN		
CAR NOTE		
COPAYS		
HEALTH INS		
CHILD CARE		
AFTER SCHOOL CARE		
		TOTAL

LIST BILLS	DUE DATE	AMOUNT

Extra Columns for Extra Bills

2. Then, add the sum of all your bills.
3. After adding up all of your bills, add up your INCOME for the month. INCOME means EVERYTHING that's COMING IN!

INCOMING INCOME	DATE RECEIVE	AMOUNT

Now you are aware of what's coming in and what's going out, and what you have LEFT!

4. Separate the bills by categorizing them by their dates. Ex: 1, 5, & 9 and 13, 18, & 20. The purpose is to place the bills that are close in numbers together, so you can KNOW what paycheck is designated to pay those bills.

LIST BILLS	DUE DATE

5. Now take the calendar and write PAY DAY for each time you get paid and/or receive any other INCOME COMING IN on an ONGOING BASIS. You can write that on the calendar referencing the day you expect to receive it.

6. Write the bills on the calendar as well. Now this makes it easier for you to decide which check will pay which bill, ON TIME or BEFORE TIME! Remember we do NOT pay late!

MONTH YEAR

MONDAY	TUESDAY	WEDNESDAY	THURSDAY	FRIDAY	SATURDAY	SUNDAY
☐	☐	☐	☐	☐	☐	☐
☐	☐	☐	☐	☐	☐	☐
☐	☐	☐	☐	☐	☐	☐
☐	☐	☐	☐	☐	☐	☐
☐	☐	☐	☐	☐	☐	☐
☐	☐	☐	☐	☐	☐	☐

Manually write the information on the calendar depending on when you start.

7. Now that you have a system in place of ADDING UP what COMES IN and SUBTRACTING what GOES OUT; Now you can decide what amount you would like to save. Then DECIDE the DATE that you want to ACCOMPLISH your GOAL.

8. DETERMINE the amount you will SAVE on a weekly or biweekly basis. This should come DIRECTLY from your check INTO your SAVINGS ACCOUNT.

9. After you DECIDE the amount that you are DETERMINED to SAVE, you must DECIDE on the amount to be withdrawn from both checks. This is setting a plan up to WIN not fail!

10. Go to HR and request a direct deposit form and fill it out. This is how you SCHEDULE IT!

GOAL AMOUNT TO SAVE	GOAL ACCOMPLISH DATE
SCHEDULED DATES	SCHEDULED AMOUNTS

In your own words write why you want to save the above amount. You must know the "reason why" in order to stay the course. This serves as a reminder to you in case you get off of track.

_____
_____
_____
_____
_____
_____
_____
_____
_____

Finalized Plan

INCOMING	OUTGOING	LEFT	SAVINGS	MISC.

Below is a monthly spending plan chart. It will help keep track of all of your monthly purchases.

PURCHASE	DATE OF PURCHASE	AMOUNT OF PURCHASE

Helpful Tips:

- Flat Rate Billing – Budget systems with your utility bills.
- Checking and Savings Accounts NOT combined.
- No Debit Card for your Savings Account.
- Preferably*Savings account with Credit Union.
- Child support in an entire different account.

1 Thessalonians 5:18 In everything give thanks: for this is the Will of God in Christ Jesus concerning you.

In some cases, we can't give thanks for everything. Maybe because everything is not good; but even in the bad GIVE THANKS! God says, the Good and the Bad will work out for your Good.

Matthew 25:21 The Master said, "Well done my Good & Faithful Servant. You have been FAITHFUL in HANDLING this SMALL amount, so NOW I will GIVE you MANY MORE RESPONSIBILITIES. Let's CELEBRATE Together!

We must also learn how to be FAITHFUL for the small things, because if not we cannot be trusted with more. God wants to see how FAITHFUL we are with MANAGING the little, so He can TRUST us with MORE Responsibilities.

- Manage = Direct Control (To be in charge of).
- Optimize = Make the BEST use of. (Most effective of).
- Navigate = Plan & Direct the route. (Create a Financial Route Plan) A way to get from one place to another.
- Examine & Execute = Test the knowledge /Carry out & put into effect. (The Plan).
- Yield = Produce & Provide. The income returns on the investment cost.

- You must be in charge over your finances and have direct control over it! Do NOT let anyone else control your finances unless it's someone that has your best interest.
- Learn how to put your money to its best use, refrain from spending it foolishly!
- You must have a Financial Route Plan telling it where to go and what to do. The plan is to help you get from where you are to where you are going.
- Just as you have to go get an examination once a year, I advise you to Examine your finances as well. Make sure the plan you set in place is working for you. If it is not, make some adjustments.
- "Produce and provide" simply explains that every investment should schedule a return.

YOU WILL NEED TO DO THE FOLLOWING:

1. Write down EVERYTHING you pay during the month (Ex: Rent, Phone, Light, Water, Gas, Life/Car Ins., Credit cards, Cellular phone, Gas (in the car), Lawn care, Household supplies, Personal hygiene supplies, Haircuts, Manicure & Pedicure). EVERYTHING!

LIST BILLS	DUE DATE	AMOUNT
RENT/MORTGAGE		
PHONE		
LIGHT		
WATER		
GAS		
LIFE/CAR INS		
FIRE/THEFT		
CABLE		
TRASH		
LAWN CARE		
PET CARE		
MANICURE/PEDICURE		
HAIRCUT/HAIR		
FOOD		
CREDIT CARD		
LOAN		
CAR NOTE		
COPAYS		
HEALTH INS		
CHILD CARE		
AFTER SCHOOL CARE		
		TOTAL

LIST BILLS	DUE DATE	AMOUNT

Extra Columns for Extra Bills

11. Then, add the sum of all your bills.
12. After adding up all of your bills, add up your INCOME for the month. INCOME means EVERYTHING that's COMING IN!

INCOMING INCOME	DATE RECEIVE	AMOUNT

Now you are aware of what's coming in and what's going out, and what you have LEFT!

13. Separate the bills by categorizing them by their dates. Ex: 1, 5, & 9 and 13, 18, & 20. The purpose is to place the bills that are close in numbers together, so you can KNOW what paycheck is designated to pay those bills.

LIST BILLS	DUE DATE

14. Now take the calendar and write PAY DAY for each time you get paid and/or receive any other INCOME COMING IN on an ONGOING BASIS. You can write that on the calendar referencing the day you expect to receive it.

15. Write the bills on the calendar as well. Now this makes it easier for you to decide which check will pay which bill, ON TIME or BEFORE TIME! Remember we do NOT pay late!

MONTH YEAR

MONDAY	TUESDAY	WEDNESDAY	THURSDAY	FRIDAY	SATURDAY	SUNDAY
☐	☐	☐	☐	☐	☐	☐
☐	☐	☐	☐	☐	☐	☐
☐	☐	☐	☐	☐	☐	☐
☐	☐	☐	☐	☐	☐	☐
☐	☐	☐	☐	☐	☐	☐
☐	☐	☐	☐	☐	☐	☐

Manually write the information on the calendar depending on when you start.

16. Now that you have a system in place of ADDING UP what COMES IN and SUBTRACTING what GOES OUT; now you can decide what amount you would like to save. Then DECIDE the DATE that you want to ACCOMPLISH your GOAL.

17. DETERMINE the amount you will SAVE on a weekly or biweekly basis. This should come DIRECTLY from your check INTO your SAVINGS ACCOUNT.

18. After you DECIDE the amount that you are DETERMINED to SAVE, you must DECIDE on the amount to be withdrawn from both checks. This is setting a plan up to WIN not fail!

19. Go to HR and request a direct deposit form and fill it out. This is how you SCHEDULE IT!

GOAL AMOUNT TO SAVE	GOAL ACCOMPLISH DATE
SCHEDULED DATES	**SCHEDULED AMOUNTS**

In your own words write why you want to save the above amount. You must know the "reason why" in order to stay the course. This serves as a reminder to you in case you get off of track.

_____
_____
_____
_____
_____
_____
_____

Finalized Plan

INCOMING	OUTGOING	LEFT	SAVINGS	MISC.

Below is a monthly spending plan chart. It will help keep track of all of your monthly purchases.

PURCHASE	DATE OF PURCHASE	AMOUNT OF PURCHASE

Helpful Tips:

- Flat Rate Billing – Budget systems with your utility bills.
- Checking and Savings Accounts NOT combined.
- No Debit Card for your Savings Account.
- Preferably*Savings account with Credit Union.
- Child support in an entire different account.

1 Thessalonians 5:18 In everything give thanks: for this is the Will of God in Christ Jesus concerning you.

In some cases, we can't give thanks for everything. Maybe because everything is not good; but even in the bad GIVE THANKS! God says, the Good and the Bad will work out for your Good.

Matthew 25:21 The Master said, "Well done my Good & Faithful Servant. You have been FAITHFUL in HANDLING this SMALL amount, so NOW I will GIVE you MANY MORE RESPONSIBILITIES. Let's CELEBRATE Together!

We must also learn how to be FAITHFUL for the small things, because if not we cannot be trusted with more. God wants to see how FAITHFUL we are with MANAGING the little, so He can TRUST us with MORE Responsibilities.

- Manage = Direct Control (To be in charge of).
- Optimize = Make the BEST use of. (Most effective of).
- Navigate = Plan & Direct the route. (Create a Financial Route Plan) A way to get from one place to another.
- Examine & Execute = Test the knowledge /Carry out & put into effect. (The Plan).
- Yield = Produce & Provide. The income returns on the investment cost.

- You must be in charge over your finances and have direct control over it! Do NOT let anyone else control your finances unless it's someone that has your best interest.
- Learn how to put your money to its best use, refrain from spending it foolishly!
- You must have a Financial Route Plan telling it where to go and what to do. The plan is to help you get from where you are to where you are going.
- Just as you have to go get an examination once a year, I advise you to Examine your finances as well. Make sure the plan you set in place is working for you. If it is not, make some adjustments.
- "Produce and provide" simply explains that every investment should schedule a return.

YOU WILL NEED TO DO THE FOLLOWING:

1. Write down EVERYTHING you pay during the month (Ex: Rent, Phone, Light, Water, Gas, Life/Car Ins., Credit cards, Cellular phone, Gas (in the car), Lawn care, Household supplies, Personal hygiene supplies, Haircuts, Manicure & Pedicure). EVERYTHING!

LIST BILLS	DUE DATE	AMOUNT
RENT/MORTGAGE		
PHONE		
LIGHT		
WATER		
GAS		
LIFE/CAR INS		
FIRE/THEFT		
CABLE		
TRASH		
LAWN CARE		
PET CARE		
MANICURE/PEDICURE		
HAIRCUT/HAIR		
FOOD		
CREDIT CARD		
LOAN		
CAR NOTE		
COPAYS		
HEALTH INS		
CHILD CARE		
AFTER SCHOOL CARE		
		TOTAL

LIST BILLS	DUE DATE	AMOUNT

Extra Columns for Extra Bills

2. Then, add the sum of all your bills.
3. After adding up all of your bills, add up your INCOME for the month. INCOME means EVERYTHING that's COMING IN!

INCOMING INCOME	DATE RECEIVE	AMOUNT

Now you are aware of what's coming in and what's going out, and what you have LEFT!

4. Separate the bills by categorizing them by their dates. Ex: 1, 5, & 9 and 13, 18, & 20. The purpose is to place the bills that are close in numbers together, so you can KNOW what paycheck is designated to pay those bills.

LIST BILLS	DUE DATE

5. Now take the calendar and write PAY DAY for each time you get paid and/or receive any other INCOME COMING IN on an ONGOING BASIS. You can write that on the calendar referencing the day you expect to receive it.

6. Write the bills on the calendar as well. Now this makes it easier for you to decide which check will pay which bill, ON TIME or BEFORE TIME! Remember we do NOT pay late!

MONTH YEAR

MONDAY	TUESDAY	WEDNESDAY	THURSDAY	FRIDAY	SATURDAY	SUNDAY
☐	☐	☐	☐	☐	☐	☐
☐	☐	☐	☐	☐	☐	☐
☐	☐	☐	☐	☐	☐	☐
☐	☐	☐	☐	☐	☐	☐
☐	☐	☐	☐	☐	☐	☐
☐	☐	☐	☐	☐	☐	☐

Manually write the information on the calendar depending on when you start.

7. Now that you have a system in place of ADDING UP what COMES IN and SUBTRACTING what GOES OUT; now you can decide what amount you would like to save. Then DECIDE the DATE that you want to ACCOMPLISH your GOAL.

8. DETERMINE the amount you will SAVE on a weekly or biweekly basis. This should come DIRECTLY from your check INTO your SAVINGS ACCOUNT.

9. After you DECIDE the amount that you are DETERMINED to SAVE, you must DECIDE on the amount to be withdrawn from both checks. This is setting a plan up to WIN not fail!

10. Go to HR and request a direct deposit form and fill it out. This is how you SCHEDULE IT!

GOAL AMOUNT TO SAVE	GOAL ACCOMPLISH DATE
SCHEDULED DATES	SCHEDULED AMOUNTS

In your own words write why you want to save the above amount. You must know the "reason why" in order to stay the course. This serves as a reminder to you in case you get off of track.

_____
_____
_____
_____
_____
_____
_____
_____

Finalized Plan

INCOMING	OUTGOING	LEFT	SAVINGS	MISC.

Below is a monthly spending plan chart. It will help keep track of all of your monthly purchases.

PURCHASE	DATE OF PURCHASE	AMOUNT OF PURCHASE

Helpful Tips:

- Flat Rate Billing – Budget systems with your utility bills.
- Checking and Savings Accounts NOT combined.
- No Debit Card for your Savings Account.
- Preferably*Savings account with Credit Union.
- Child support in an entire different account.

1 Thessalonians 5:18 In everything give thanks: for this is the Will of God in Christ Jesus concerning you.

In some cases, we can't give thanks for everything. Maybe because everything is not good; but even in the bad GIVE THANKS! God says, the Good and the Bad will work out for your Good.

Matthew 25:21 The Master said, "Well done my Good & Faithful Servant. You have been FAITHFUL in HANDLING this SMALL amount, so NOW I will GIVE you MANY MORE RESPONSIBILITIES. Let's CELEBRATE Together!

We must also learn how to be FAITHFUL for the small things, because if not we cannot be trusted with more. God wants to see how FAITHFUL we are with MANAGING the little, so He can TRUST us with MORE Responsibilities.

- Manage = Direct Control (To be in charge of).
- Optimize = Make the BEST use of. (Most effective of).
- Navigate = Plan & Direct the route. (Create a Financial Route Plan) A way to get from one place to another.
- Examine & Execute = Test the knowledge /Carry out & put into effect. (The Plan).
- Yield = Produce & Provide. The income returns on the investment cost.

- You must be in charge over your finances and have direct control over it! Do NOT let anyone else control your finances unless it's someone that has your best interest.
- Learn how to put your money to its best use, refrain from spending it foolishly!
- You must have a Financial Route Plan telling it where to go and what to do. The plan is to help you get from where you are to where you are going.
- Just as you have to go get an examination once a year, I advise you to Examine your finances as well. Make sure the plan you set in place is working for you. If it is not, make some adjustments.
- "Produce and provide" simply explains that every investment should schedule a return.

YOU WILL NEED TO DO THE FOLLOWING:

1. Write down EVERYTHING you pay during the month (Ex: Rent, Phone, Light, Water, Gas, Life/Car Ins., Credit cards, Cellular phone, Gas (in the car), Lawn care, Household supplies, Personal hygiene supplies, Haircuts, Manicure & Pedicure). EVERYTHING!

LIST BILLS	DUE DATE	AMOUNT
RENT/MORTGAGE		
PHONE		
LIGHT		
WATER		
GAS		
LIFE/CAR INS		
FIRE/THEFT		
CABLE		
TRASH		
LAWN CARE		
PET CARE		
MANICURE/PEDICURE		
HAIRCUT/HAIR		
FOOD		
CREDIT CARD		
LOAN		
CAR NOTE		
COPAYS		
HEALTH INS		
CHILD CARE		
AFTER SCHOOL CARE		
		TOTAL

LIST BILLS	DUE DATE	AMOUNT

Extra Columns for Extra Bills

2. Then, add the sum of all your bills.
3. After adding up all of your bills, add up your INCOME for the month. INCOME means EVERYTHING that's COMING IN!

INCOMING INCOME	DATE RECEIVE	AMOUNT

Now you are aware of what's coming in and what's going out, and what you have LEFT!

4. Separate the bills by categorizing them by their dates. Ex: 1, 5, & 9 and 13, 18, & 20. The purpose is to place the bills that are close in numbers together, so you can KNOW what paycheck is designated to pay those bills.

LIST BILLS	DUE DATE

5. Now take the calendar and write PAY DAY for each time you get paid and/or receive any other INCOME COMING IN on an ONGOING BASIS. You can write that on the calendar referencing the day you expect to receive it.

6. Write the bills on the calendar as well. Now this makes it easier for you to decide which check will pay which bill, ON TIME or BEFORE TIME! Remember we do NOT pay late!

MONTH YEAR

MONDAY	TUESDAY	WEDNESDAY	THURSDAY	FRIDAY	SATURDAY	SUNDAY
☐	☐	☐	☐	☐	☐	☐
☐	☐	☐	☐	☐	☐	☐
☐	☐	☐	☐	☐	☐	☐
☐	☐	☐	☐	☐	☐	☐
☐	☐	☐	☐	☐	☐	☐
☐	☐	☐	☐	☐	☐	☐

Manually write the information on the calendar depending on when you start.

7. Now that you have a system in place of ADDING UP what COMES IN and SUBTRACTING what GOES OUT; now you can decide what amount you would like to save. Then DECIDE the DATE that you want to ACCOMPLISH your GOAL.

8. DETERMINE the amount you will SAVE on a weekly or biweekly basis. This should come DIRECTLY from your check INTO your SAVINGS ACCOUNT.

9. After you DECIDE the amount that you are DETERMINED to SAVE, you must DECIDE on the amount to be withdrawn from both checks. This is setting a plan up to WIN not fail!

10. Go to HR and request a direct deposit form and fill it out. This is how you SCHEDULE IT!

GOAL AMOUNT TO SAVE	GOAL ACCOMPLISH DATE
SCHEDULED DATES	**SCHEDULED AMOUNTS**

In your own words write why you want to save the above amount. You must know the "reason why" in order to stay the course. This serves as a reminder to you in case you get off of track.

_____
_____
_____
_____
_____
_____
_____
_____

Finalized Plan

INCOMING	OUTGOING	LEFT	SAVINGS	MISC.

Below is a monthly spending plan chart. It will help keep track of all of your monthly purchases.

PURCHASE	DATE OF PURCHASE	AMOUNT OF PURCHASE

Helpful Tips:

- Flat Rate Billing – Budget systems with your utility bills.
- Checking and Savings Accounts NOT combined.
- No Debit Card for your Savings Account.
- Preferably*Savings account with Credit Union.
- Child support in an entire different account.

1 Thessalonians 5:18 In everything give thanks: for this is the Will of God in Christ Jesus concerning you.

In some cases, we can't give thanks for everything. Maybe because everything is not good; but even in the bad GIVE THANKS! God says, the Good and the Bad will work out for your Good.

Matthew 25:21 The Master said, "Well done my Good & Faithful Servant. You have been FAITHFUL in HANDLING this SMALL amount, so NOW I will GIVE you MANY MORE RESPONSIBILITIES. Let's CELEBRATE Together!

We must also learn how to be FAITHFUL for the small things, because if not we cannot be trusted with more. God wants to see how FAITHFUL we are with MANAGING the little, so He can TRUST us with MORE Responsibilities.

- Manage = Direct Control (To be in charge of).
- Optimize = Make the BEST use of. (Most effective of).
- Navigate = Plan & Direct the route. (Create a Financial Route Plan) A way to get from one place to another.
- Examine & Execute = Test the knowledge /Carry out & put into effect. (The Plan).
- Yield = Produce & Provide. The income returns on the investment cost.

- You must be in charge over your finances and have direct control over it! Do NOT let anyone else control your finances unless it's someone that has your best interest.
- Learn how to put your money to its best use, refrain from spending it foolishly!
- You must have a Financial Route Plan telling it where to go and what to do. The plan is to help you get from where you are to where you are going.
- Just as you have to go get an examination once a year, I advise you to Examine your finances as well. Make sure the plan you set in place is working for you. If it is not, make some adjustments.
- "Produce and provide" simply explains that every investment should schedule a return.

YOU WILL NEED TO DO THE FOLLOWING:

1. Write down EVERYTHING you pay during the month (Ex: Rent, Phone, Light, Water, Gas, Life/Car Ins., Credit cards, Cellular phone, Gas (in the car), Lawn care, Household supplies, Personal hygiene supplies, Haircuts, Manicure & Pedicure). EVERYTHING!

LIST BILLS	DUE DATE	AMOUNT
RENT/MORTGAGE		
PHONE		
LIGHT		
WATER		
GAS		
LIFE/CAR INS		
FIRE/THEFT		
CABLE		
TRASH		
LAWN CARE		
PET CARE		
MANICURE/PEDICURE		
HAIRCUT/HAIR		
FOOD		
CREDIT CARD		
LOAN		
CAR NOTE		
COPAYS		
HEALTH INS		
CHILD CARE		
AFTER SCHOOL CARE		
		TOTAL

LIST BILLS	DUE DATE	AMOUNT

Extra Columns for Extra Bills

2. Then, add the sum of all your bills.
3. After adding up all of your bills, add up your INCOME for the month. INCOME means EVERYTHING that's COMING IN!

INCOMING INCOME	DATE RECEIVE	AMOUNT

Now you are aware of what's coming in and what's going out, and what you have LEFT!

4. Separate the bills by categorizing them by their dates. Ex: 1, 5, & 9 and 13, 18, & 20. The purpose is to place the bills that are close in numbers together, so you can KNOW what paycheck is designated to pay those bills.

LIST BILLS	DUE DATE

5. Now take the calendar and write PAY DAY for each time you get paid and/or receive any other INCOME COMING IN on an ONGOING BASIS. You can write that on the calendar referencing the day you expect to receive it.

6. Write the bills on the calendar as well. Now this makes it easier for you to decide which check will pay which bill, ON TIME or BEFORE TIME! Remember we do NOT pay late!

MONTH YEAR

MONDAY	TUESDAY	WEDNESDAY	THURSDAY	FRIDAY	SATURDAY	SUNDAY
☐	☐	☐	☐	☐	☐	☐
☐	☐	☐	☐	☐	☐	☐
☐	☐	☐	☐	☐	☐	☐
☐	☐	☐	☐	☐	☐	☐
☐	☐	☐	☐	☐	☐	☐
☐	☐	☐	☐	☐	☐	☐

Manually write the information on the calendar depending on when you start.

7. Now that you have a system in place of ADDING UP what COMES IN and SUBTRACTING what GOES OUT; now you can decide what amount you would like to save. Then DECIDE the DATE that you want to ACCOMPLISH your GOAL.

8. DETERMINE the amount you will SAVE on a weekly or biweekly basis. This should come DIRECTLY from your check INTO your SAVINGS ACCOUNT.

9. After you DECIDE the amount that you are DETERMINED to SAVE, you must DECIDE on the amount to be withdrawn from both checks. This is setting a plan up to WIN not fail!

10. Go to HR and request a direct deposit form and fill it out. This is how you SCHEDULE IT!

GOAL AMOUNT TO SAVE	GOAL ACCOMPLISH DATE
SCHEDULED DATES	SCHEDULED AMOUNTS

In your own words write why you want to save the above amount. You must know the "reason why" in order to stay the course. This serves as a reminder to you in case you get off of track.

_____
_____
_____
_____
_____
_____
_____
_____

Finalized Plan

INCOMING	OUTGOING	LEFT	SAVINGS	MISC.

Below is a monthly spending plan chart. It will help keep track of all of your monthly purchases.

PURCHASE	DATE OF PURCHASE	AMOUNT OF PURCHASE

Helpful Tips:

- Flat Rate Billing – Budget systems with your utility bills.
- Checking and Savings Accounts NOT combined.
- No Debit Card for your Savings Account.
- Preferably*Savings account with Credit Union.
- Child support in an entire different account.

1 Thessalonians 5:18 In everything give thanks: for this is the Will of God in Christ Jesus concerning you.

In some cases, we can't give thanks for everything. Maybe because everything is not good; but even in the bad GIVE THANKS! God says, the Good and the Bad will work out for your Good.

Matthew 25:21 The Master said, "Well done my Good & Faithful Servant. You have been FAITHFUL in HANDLING this SMALL amount, so NOW I will GIVE you MANY MORE RESPONSIBILITIES. Let's CELEBRATE Together!

We must also learn how to be FAITHFUL for the small things, because if not we cannot be trusted with more. God wants to see how FAITHFUL we are with MANAGING the little, so He can TRUST us with MORE Responsibilities.

- Manage = Direct Control (To be in charge of).
- Optimize = Make the BEST use of. (Most effective of).
- Navigate = Plan & Direct the route. (Create a Financial Route Plan) A way to get from one place to another.
- Examine & Execute = Test the knowledge /Carry out & put into effect. (The Plan).
- Yield = Produce & Provide. The income returns on the investment cost.

- You must be in charge over your finances and have direct control over it! Do NOT let anyone else control your finances unless it's someone that has your best interest.
- Learn how to put your money to its best use, refrain from spending it foolishly!
- You must have a Financial Route Plan telling it where to go and what to do. The plan is to help you get from where you are to where you are going.
- Just as you have to go get an examination once a year, I advise you to Examine your finances as well. Make sure the plan you set in place is working for you. If it is not, make some adjustments.
- "Produce and provide" simply explains that every investment should schedule a return.

YOU WILL NEED TO DO THE FOLLOWING:

1. Write down EVERYTHING you pay during the month (Ex: Rent, Phone, Light, Water, Gas, Life/Car Ins., Credit cards, Cellular phone, Gas (in the car), Lawn care, Household supplies, Personal hygiene supplies, Haircuts, Manicure & Pedicure). EVERYTHING!

LIST BILLS	DUE DATE	AMOUNT
RENT/MORTGAGE		
PHONE		
LIGHT		
WATER		
GAS		
LIFE/CAR INS		
FIRE/THEFT		
CABLE		
TRASH		
LAWN CARE		
PET CARE		
MANICURE/PEDICURE		
HAIRCUT/HAIR		
FOOD		
CREDIT CARD		
LOAN		
CAR NOTE		
COPAYS		
HEALTH INS		
CHILD CARE		
AFTER SCHOOL CARE		
		TOTAL

LIST BILLS	DUE DATE	AMOUNT

Extra Columns for Extra Bills

2. Then, add the sum of all your bills.
3. After adding up all of your bills, add up your INCOME for the month. INCOME means EVERYTHING that's COMING IN!

INCOMING INCOME	DATE RECEIVE	AMOUNT

Now you are aware of what's coming in and what's going out, and what you have LEFT!

4. Separate the bills by categorizing them by their dates. Ex: 1, 5, & 9 and 13, 18, & 20. The purpose is to place the bills that are close in numbers together, so you can KNOW what paycheck is designated to pay those bills.

LIST BILLS	DUE DATE

5. Now take the calendar and write PAY DAY for each time you get paid and/or receive any other INCOME COMING IN on an ONGOING BASIS. You can write that on the calendar referencing the day you expect to receive it.

6. Write the bills on the calendar as well. Now this makes it easier for you to decide which check will pay which bill, ON TIME or BEFORE TIME! Remember we do NOT pay late!

MONTH YEAR

MONDAY	TUESDAY	WEDNESDAY	THURSDAY	FRIDAY	SATURDAY	SUNDAY
☐	☐	☐	☐	☐	☐	☐
☐	☐	☐	☐	☐	☐	☐
☐	☐	☐	☐	☐	☐	☐
☐	☐	☐	☐	☐	☐	☐
☐	☐	☐	☐	☐	☐	☐
☐	☐	☐	☐	☐	☐	☐

Manually write the information on the calendar depending on when you start.

7. Now that you have a system in place of ADDING UP what COMES IN and SUBTRACTING what GOES OUT; now you can decide what amount you would like to save. Then DECIDE the DATE that you want to ACCOMPLISH your GOAL.

8. DETERMINE the amount you will SAVE on a weekly or biweekly basis. This should come DIRECTLY from your check INTO your SAVINGS ACCOUNT.

9. After you DECIDE the amount that you are DETERMINED to SAVE, you must DECIDE on the amount to be withdrawn from both checks. This is setting a plan up to WIN not fail!

10. Go to HR and request a direct deposit form and fill it out. This is how you SCHEDULE IT!

GOAL AMOUNT TO SAVE	GOAL ACCOMPLISH DATE
SCHEDULED DATES	SCHEDULED AMOUNTS

In your own words write why you want to save the above amount. You must know the "reason why" in order to stay the course. This serves as a reminder to you in case you get off of track.

_____
_____
_____
_____
_____
_____
_____
_____

Finalized Plan

INCOMING	OUTGOING	LEFT	SAVINGS	MISC.

Below is a monthly spending plan chart. It will help keep track of all of your monthly purchases.

PURCHASE	DATE OF PURCHASE	AMOUNT OF PURCHASE

Helpful Tips:

- Flat Rate Billing – Budget systems with your utility bills.
- Checking and Savings Accounts NOT combined.
- No Debit Card for your Savings Account.
- Preferably*Savings account with Credit Union.
- Child support in an entire different account.

1 Thessalonians 5:18 In everything give thanks: for this is the Will of God in Christ Jesus concerning you.

In some cases, we can't give thanks for everything. Maybe because everything is not good; but even in the bad GIVE THANKS! God says, the Good and the Bad will work out for your Good.

Matthew 25:21 The Master said, "Well done my Good & Faithful Servant. You have been FAITHFUL in HANDLING this SMALL amount, so NOW I will GIVE you MANY MORE RESPONSIBILITIES. Let's CELEBRATE Together!

We must also learn how to be FAITHFUL for the small things, because if not we cannot be trusted with more. God wants to see how FAITHFUL we are with MANAGING the little, so He can TRUST us with MORE Responsibilities.

- Manage = Direct Control (To be in charge of).
- Optimize = Make the BEST use of. (Most effective of).
- Navigate = Plan & Direct the route. (Create a Financial Route Plan) A way to get from one place to another.
- Examine & Execute = Test the knowledge /Carry out & put into effect. (The Plan).
- Yield = Produce & Provide. The income returns on the investment cost.

- You must be in charge over your finances and have direct control over it! Do NOT let anyone else control your finances unless it's someone that has your best interest.
- Learn how to put your money to its best use, refrain from spending it foolishly!
- You must have a Financial Route Plan telling it where to go and what to do. The plan is to help you get from where you are to where you are going.
- Just as you have to go get an examination once a year, I advise you to Examine your finances as well. Make sure the plan you set in place is working for you. If it is not, make some adjustments.
- "Produce and provide" simply explains that every investment should schedule a return.

YOU WILL NEED TO DO THE FOLLOWING:

1. Write down EVERYTHING you pay during the month (Ex: Rent, Phone, Light, Water, Gas, Life/Car Ins., Credit cards, Cellular phone, Gas (in the car), Lawn care, Household supplies, Personal hygiene supplies, Haircuts, Manicure & Pedicure). EVERYTHING!

LIST BILLS	DUE DATE	AMOUNT
RENT/MORTGAGE		
PHONE		
LIGHT		
WATER		
GAS		
LIFE/CAR INS		
FIRE/THEFT		
CABLE		
TRASH		
LAWN CARE		
PET CARE		
MANICURE/PEDICURE		
HAIRCUT/HAIR		
FOOD		
CREDIT CARD		
LOAN		
CAR NOTE		
COPAYS		
HEALTH INS		
CHILD CARE		
AFTER SCHOOL CARE		
		TOTAL

LIST BILLS	DUE DATE	AMOUNT

Extra Columns for Extra Bills

2. Then, add the sum of all your bills.
3. After adding up all of your bills, add up your INCOME for the month. INCOME means EVERYTHING that's COMING IN!

INCOMING INCOME	DATE RECEIVE	AMOUNT

Now you are aware of what's coming in and what's going out, and what you have LEFT!

4. Separate the bills by categorizing them by their dates. Ex: 1, 5, & 9 and 13, 18, & 20. The purpose is to place the bills that are close in numbers together, so you can KNOW what paycheck is designated to pay those bills.

LIST BILLS	DUE DATE

5. Now take the calendar and write PAY DAY for each time you get paid and/or receive any other INCOME COMING IN on an ONGOING BASIS. You can write that on the calendar referencing the day you expect to receive it.

6. Write the bills on the calendar as well. Now this makes it easier for you to decide which check will pay which bill, ON TIME or BEFORE TIME! Remember we do NOT pay late!

MONTH YEAR

MONDAY	TUESDAY	WEDNESDAY	THURSDAY	FRIDAY	SATURDAY	SUNDAY
☐	☐	☐	☐	☐	☐	☐
☐	☐	☐	☐	☐	☐	☐
☐	☐	☐	☐	☐	☐	☐
☐	☐	☐	☐	☐	☐	☐
☐	☐	☐	☐	☐	☐	☐
☐	☐	☐	☐	☐	☐	☐

Manually write the information on the calendar depending on when you start.

7. Now that you have a system in place of ADDING UP what COMES IN and SUBTRACTING what GOES OUT; now you can decide what amount you would like to save. Then DECIDE the DATE that you want to ACCOMPLISH your GOAL.

8. DETERMINE the amount you will SAVE on a weekly or biweekly basis. This should come DIRECTLY from your check INTO your SAVINGS ACCOUNT.

9. After you DECIDE the amount that you are DETERMINED to SAVE, you must DECIDE on the amount to be withdrawn from both checks. This is setting a plan up to WIN not fail!

10. Go to HR and request a direct deposit form and fill it out. This is how you SCHEDULE IT!

GOAL AMOUNT TO SAVE	GOAL ACCOMPLISH DATE
SCHEDULED DATES	SCHEDULED AMOUNTS

In your own words write why you want to save the above amount. You must know the "reason why" in order to stay the course. This serves as a reminder to you in case you get off of track.

_____
_____
_____
_____
_____
_____
_____
_____

Finalized Plan

INCOMING	OUTGOING	LEFT	SAVINGS	MISC.

Below is a monthly spending plan chart. It will help keep track of all of your monthly purchases.

PURCHASE	DATE OF PURCHASE	AMOUNT OF PURCHASE

Helpful Tips:

- Flat Rate Billing – Budget systems with your utility bills.
- Checking and Savings Accounts NOT combined.
- No Debit Card for your Savings Account.
- Preferably*Savings account with Credit Union.
- Child support in an entire different account.

1 Thessalonians 5:18 In everything give thanks: for this is the Will of God in Christ Jesus concerning you.

In some cases, we can't give thanks for everything. Maybe because everything is not good; but even in the bad GIVE THANKS! God says, the Good and the Bad will work out for your Good.

Matthew 25:21 The Master said, "Well done my Good & Faithful Servant. You have been FAITHFUL in HANDLING this SMALL amount, so NOW I will GIVE you MANY MORE RESPONSIBILITIES. Let's CELEBRATE Together!

We must also learn how to be FAITHFUL for the small things, because if not we cannot be trusted with more. God wants to see how FAITHFUL we are with MANAGING the little, so He can TRUST us with MORE Responsibilities.

- Manage = Direct Control (To be in charge of).
- Optimize = Make the BEST use of. (Most effective of).
- Navigate = Plan & Direct the route. (Create a Financial Route Plan) A way to get from one place to another.
- Examine & Execute = Test the knowledge /Carry out & put into effect. (The Plan).
- Yield = Produce & Provide. The income returns on the investment cost.

- You must be in charge over your finances and have direct control over it! Do NOT let anyone else control your finances unless it's someone that has your best interest.
- Learn how to put your money to its best use, refrain from spending it foolishly!
- You must have a Financial Route Plan telling it where to go and what to do. The plan is to help you get from where you are to where you are going.
- Just as you have to go get an examination once a year, I advise you to Examine your finances as well. Make sure the plan you set in place is working for you. If it is not, make some adjustments.
- "Produce and provide" simply explains that every investment should schedule a return.

YOU WILL NEED TO DO THE FOLLOWING:

1. Write down EVERYTHING you pay during the month (Ex: Rent, Phone, Light, Water, Gas, Life/Car Ins., Credit cards, Cellular phone, Gas (in the car), Lawn care, Household supplies, Personal hygiene supplies, Haircuts, Manicure & Pedicure). EVERYTHING!

LIST BILLS	DUE DATE	AMOUNT
RENT/MORTGAGE		
PHONE		
LIGHT		
WATER		
GAS		
LIFE/CAR INS		
FIRE/THEFT		
CABLE		
TRASH		
LAWN CARE		
PET CARE		
MANICURE/PEDICURE		
HAIRCUT/HAIR		
FOOD		
CREDIT CARD		
LOAN		
CAR NOTE		
COPAYS		
HEALTH INS		
CHILD CARE		
AFTER SCHOOL CARE		
		TOTAL

LIST BILLS	DUE DATE	AMOUNT

Extra Columns for Extra Bills

2. Then, add the sum of all your bills.
3. After adding up all of your bills, add up your INCOME for the month. INCOME means EVERYTHING that's COMING IN!

INCOMING INCOME	DATE RECEIVE	AMOUNT

Now you are aware of what's coming in and what's going out, and what you have LEFT!

4. Separate the bills by categorizing them by their dates. Ex: 1, 5, & 9 and 13, 18, & 20. The purpose is to place the bills that are close in numbers together, so you can KNOW what paycheck is designated to pay those bills.

LIST BILLS	DUE DATE

5. Now take the calendar and write PAY DAY for each time you get paid and/or receive any other INCOME COMING IN on an ONGOING BASIS. You can write that on the calendar referencing the day you expect to receive it.

6. Write the bills on the calendar as well. Now this makes it easier for you to decide which check will pay which bill, ON TIME or BEFORE TIME! Remember we do NOT pay late!

MONTH YEAR

MONDAY	TUESDAY	WEDNESDAY	THURSDAY	FRIDAY	SATURDAY	SUNDAY
☐	☐	☐	☐	☐	☐	☐
☐	☐	☐	☐	☐	☐	☐
☐	☐	☐	☐	☐	☐	☐
☐	☐	☐	☐	☐	☐	☐
☐	☐	☐	☐	☐	☐	☐
☐	☐	☐	☐	☐	☐	☐

Manually write the information on the calendar depending on when you start.

7. Now that you have a system in place of ADDING UP what COMES IN and SUBTRACTING what GOES OUT; now you can decide what amount you would like to save. Then DECIDE the DATE that you want to ACCOMPLISH your GOAL.

8. DETERMINE the amount you will SAVE on a weekly or biweekly basis. This should come DIRECTLY from your check INTO your SAVINGS ACCOUNT.

9. After you DECIDE the amount that you are DETERMINED to SAVE, you must DECIDE on the amount to be withdrawn from both checks. This is setting a plan up to WIN not fail!

10. Go to HR and request a direct deposit form and fill it out. This is how you SCHEDULE IT!

GOAL AMOUNT TO SAVE	GOAL ACCOMPLISH DATE
SCHEDULED DATES	SCHEDULED AMOUNTS

In your own words write why you want to save the above amount. You must know the "reason why" in order to stay the course. This serves as a reminder to you in case you get off of track.

_____
_____
_____
_____
_____
_____
_____
_____

Finalized Plan

INCOMING	OUTGOING	LEFT	SAVINGS	MISC.

Below is a monthly spending plan chart. It will help keep track of all of your monthly purchases.

PURCHASE	DATE OF PURCHASE	AMOUNT OF PURCHASE

Helpful Tips:

- Flat Rate Billing – Budget systems with your utility bills.
- Checking and Savings Accounts NOT combined.
- No Debit Card for your Savings Account.
- Preferably*Savings account with Credit Union.
- Child support in an entire different account.

1 Thessalonians 5:18 In everything give thanks: for this is the Will of God in Christ Jesus concerning you.

In some cases, we can't give thanks for everything. Maybe because everything is not good; but even in the bad GIVE THANKS! God says, the Good and the Bad will work out for your Good.

Matthew 25:21 The Master said, "Well done my Good & Faithful Servant. You have been FAITHFUL in HANDLING this SMALL amount, so NOW I will GIVE you MANY MORE RESPONSIBILITIES. Let's CELEBRATE Together!

We must also learn how to be FAITHFUL for the small things, because if not we cannot be trusted with more. God wants to see how FAITHFUL we are with MANAGING the little, so He can TRUST us with MORE Responsibilities.

- Manage = Direct Control (To be in charge of).
- Optimize = Make the BEST use of. (Most effective of).
- Navigate = Plan & Direct the route. (Create a Financial Route Plan) A way to get from one place to another.
- Examine & Execute = Test the knowledge /Carry out & put into effect. (The Plan).
- Yield = Produce & Provide. The income returns on the investment cost.

- You must be in charge over your finances and have direct control over it! Do NOT let anyone else control your finances unless it's someone that has your best interest.
- Learn how to put your money to its best use, refrain from spending it foolishly!
- You must have a Financial Route Plan telling it where to go and what to do. The plan is to help you get from where you are to where you are going.
- Just as you have to go get an examination once a year, I advise you to Examine your finances as well. Make sure the plan you set in place is working for you. If it is not, make some adjustments.
- "Produce and provide" simply explains that every investment should schedule a return.

YOU WILL NEED TO DO THE FOLLOWING:

1. Write down EVERYTHING you pay during the month (Ex: Rent, Phone, Light, Water, Gas, Life/Car Ins., Credit cards, Cellular phone, Gas (in the car), Lawn care, Household supplies, Personal hygiene supplies, Haircuts, Manicure & Pedicure). EVERYTHING!

LIST BILLS	DUE DATE	AMOUNT
RENT/MORTGAGE		
PHONE		
LIGHT		
WATER		
GAS		
LIFE/CAR INS		
FIRE/THEFT		
CABLE		
TRASH		
LAWN CARE		
PET CARE		
MANICURE/PEDICURE		
HAIRCUT/HAIR		
FOOD		
CREDIT CARD		
LOAN		
CAR NOTE		
COPAYS		
HEALTH INS		
CHILD CARE		
AFTER SCHOOL CARE		
		TOTAL

LIST BILLS	DUE DATE	AMOUNT

Extra Columns for Extra Bills

2. Then, add the sum of all your bills.
3. After adding up all of your bills, add up your INCOME for the month. INCOME means EVERYTHING that's COMING IN!

INCOMING INCOME	DATE RECEIVE	AMOUNT

Now you are aware of what's coming in and what's going out, and what you have LEFT!

4. Separate the bills by categorizing them by their dates. Ex: 1, 5, & 9 and 13, 18, & 20. The purpose is to place the bills that are close in numbers together, so you can KNOW what paycheck is designated to pay those bills.

LIST BILLS	DUE DATE

5. Now take the calendar and write PAY DAY for each time you get paid and/or receive any other INCOME COMING IN on an ONGOING BASIS. You can write that on the calendar referencing the day you expect to receive it.

6. Write the bills on the calendar as well. Now this makes it easier for you to decide which check will pay which bill, ON TIME or BEFORE TIME! Remember we do NOT pay late!

MONTH YEAR

MONDAY	TUESDAY	WEDNESDAY	THURSDAY	FRIDAY	SATURDAY	SUNDAY
☐	☐	☐	☐	☐	☐	☐
☐	☐	☐	☐	☐	☐	☐
☐	☐	☐	☐	☐	☐	☐
☐	☐	☐	☐	☐	☐	☐
☐	☐	☐	☐	☐	☐	☐
☐	☐	☐	☐	☐	☐	☐

Manually write the information on the calendar depending on when you start.

7. Now that you have a system in place of ADDING UP what COMES IN and SUBTRACTING what GOES OUT; now you can decide what amount you would like to save. Then DECIDE the DATE that you want to ACCOMPLISH your GOAL.

8. DETERMINE the amount you will SAVE on a weekly or biweekly basis. This should come DIRECTLY from your check INTO your SAVINGS ACCOUNT.

9. After you DECIDE the amount that you are DETERMINED to SAVE, you must DECIDE on the amount to be withdrawn from both checks. This is setting a plan up to WIN not fail!

10. Go to HR and request a direct deposit form and fill it out. This is how you SCHEDULE IT!

GOAL AMOUNT TO SAVE	GOAL ACCOMPLISH DATE
SCHEDULED DATES	SCHEDULED AMOUNTS

In your own words write why you want to save the above amount. You must know the "reason why" in order to stay the course. This serves as a reminder to you in case you get off of track.

_____
_____
_____
_____
_____
_____
_____
_____

Finalized Plan

INCOMING	OUTGOING	LEFT	SAVINGS	MISC.

Below is a monthly spending plan chart. It will help keep track of all of your monthly purchases.

PURCHASE	DATE OF PURCHASE	AMOUNT OF PURCHASE

Helpful Tips:

- Flat Rate Billing – Budget systems with your utility bills.
- Checking and Savings Accounts NOT combined.
- No Debit Card for your Savings Account.
- Preferably*Savings account with Credit Union.
- Child support in an entire different account.

1 Thessalonians 5:18 In everything give thanks: for this is the Will of God in Christ Jesus concerning you.

In some cases, we can't give thanks for everything. Maybe because everything is not good; but even in the bad GIVE THANKS! God says, the Good and the Bad will work out for your Good.

Matthew 25:21 The Master said, "Well done my Good & Faithful Servant. You have been FAITHFUL in HANDLING this SMALL amount, so NOW I will GIVE you MANY MORE RESPONSIBILITIES. Let's CELEBRATE Together!

We must also learn how to be FAITHFUL for the small things, because if not we cannot be trusted with more. God wants to see how FAITHFUL we are with MANAGING the little, so He can TRUST us with MORE Responsibilities.

- Manage = Direct Control (To be in charge of).
- Optimize = Make the BEST use of. (Most effective of).
- Navigate = Plan & Direct the route. (Create a Financial Route Plan) A way to get from one place to another.
- Examine & Execute = Test the knowledge /Carry out & put into effect. (The Plan).
- Yield = Produce & Provide. The income returns on the investment cost.

- You must be in charge over your finances and have direct control over it! Do NOT let anyone else control your finances unless it's someone that has your best interest.
- Learn how to put your money to its best use, refrain from spending it foolishly!
- You must have a Financial Route Plan telling it where to go and what to do. The plan is to help you get from where you are to where you are going.
- Just as you have to go get an examination once a year, I advise you to Examine your finances as well. Make sure the plan you set in place is working for you. If it is not, make some adjustments.
- "Produce and provide" simply explains that every investment should schedule a return.

In closing,

God does everything in decency and in order. He said that His word shall not return unto Him void. If you delight yourself in Him, He shall give you the desires of your heart. He said, "As you bring the whole tithe into the storehouse that His house may have food, see won't He open up the floodgates of Heaven and pour you out so much blessing that you won't have room enough to receive.

The overflow of blessings and miracles shall fall upon your land. You shall reap what you sow. Sow your first fruits in Jesus the Christ, sow your ten percent and watch God provide the increase. Always remain faithful over the few so that He will see you as responsible and appreciative for the more. To whom much is given, much is required.

Blessings,

Shakisha Edness

Author/Money Manager Coach

www.ingramcontent.com/pod-product-compliance
Lightning Source LLC
Chambersburg PA
CBHW080708190526
45169CB00006B/2298